CREATIVE STENCILLING

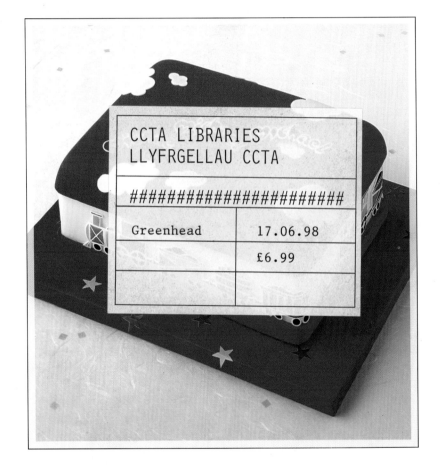

SARAH GLEAVE

BASED ON · CITY AND GUILDS SUGARCRAFT COURSE

MEREHURST

To Mum and Dad

Thank you John, Kenzie, Jessica, Jean and Derek, and Adrian Westrope for your continuous help and support.

Published in 1995 by Merehurst Limited, Ferry House, 51 – 57 Lacy Road, Putney, London SW15 1PR

ISBN 1-85391-495-9

Managing Editor Bridget Jones
Edited by Alison Leach
Designed by Jo Tapper
Photography by Graham Tann
Colour separation by Global Colour, Malaysia
Printed by Wing King Tong, Hong Kong

The author and publishers would like to thank the following for their assistance:
Anniversary House (Cake Decorations) Ltd., Unit 16, Elliott Road, West Howe Industrial Estate, Bournemouth, BH11 8LZ;
Cake Art Ltd., Venture Way, Crown Estate Priorswood, Taunton, Somerset TA2 8DE;
Craigmiller, Craigmiller House, Stadium Road, Bromborough, Wirral, Merseyside, L62 3NU;
Creative Stencil Designs, Easter Poldar Farm, Thornhill, Stirling, Scotland, FK8 3QT
(for pre-cut stencils and equipment);
Guy, Paul & Co. Ltd., Unit B4, Foundary Way, Little End Road, Eaton Socon, Cambridge, PE19 3JH;
Squires Kitchen, Squires House, 3 Waverley Lane, Farnham, Surrey, GU9 8BB
(for food colourings and sugars).

NOTES ON USING THE RECIPES
For all recipes, quantities are given in metric, Imperial and cup measurements. Follow one set of measures only as they are not interchangeable. Standard 5ml teaspoons (tsp) and 15ml tablespoons (tbsp) are used. Australian readers, whose tablespoons measure 20ml, should adjust quantities accordingly. All spoon measures are assumed to be level unless otherwise stated.
Eggs are a standard size 3 (medium) unless otherwise stated.

CONTENTS

INTRODUCTION

Stencilling is by no means a new concept; it has been used as a quick and effective form of decoration for many years, particularly within the bakery trade. It has mostly been associated with royal icing, but the use of dusting powders (petal dusts/blossom tints) has completely changed the application of stencils. The results are colourful and dramatic, and offer endless variations on a theme.

Stencilling with colours and creating stencilled decorations off the main surface of the cake have made me develop a totally different approach to the technique. The decorations have immediately become 3-D as a result.

The aim of this book is to demonstrate how versatile the technique can be. Airbrushing and royal icing have also been included to show the extensive range of applications possible when working with stencils. As a quick-and-easy decoration stencilling is ideal for achieving fast results. It is also a perfect technique for producing more than one cake of the same design. Another advantage is that the cakes can be decorated well in advance of when they are required. To complement the technique, I have included some simple suggestions for finishing the decoration of the cake and cake boards.

The full-colour step-by-step instructions and expert advice will enable you to improve and develop your stencilling skills. This book shows how most subjects can be adapted and reproduced in stencil form, so that it is possible to create your own designs.

Writing this book has inspired me even more to broaden the potential of stencilling. Once you have mastered the technique, I hope you will become as addicted as I am!

BASIC TECHNIQUES AND RECIPES

*S*ugarcrafters who have some experience will already have most of the necessary equipment for stencilling. All these items are available from cake decorating or art and craft supply shops. The photograph on the opposite page illustrates the following, more useful, items: non-stick rolling pin and board; scalpel or craft knife and spare no. 11 blades; cutting mat; acetate; polyester film or stencilling film; palette knife; airbrush; waterproof pen or chinagraph pencil; range of paintbrushes with synthetic bristles as they hold the colour better when dusting; edible food colourings – dusting powder (petal dust/blossom tint), paste, and liquid; cornflour (cornstarch); white vegetable fat (shortening); glass-headed pins; thick card; puffer.

STENCILLING PASTE

225g (8 oz/1½ cups) icing (confectioners')
sugar, sifted
15ml (1 tbsp) gum tragacanth
5ml (1 tsp) liquid glucose (clear corn syrup)
30ml (2 tbsp) cold water
250g (8 oz) pastello or sugarpaste

● Sift the icing sugar and gum tragacanth into a mixing bowl. Make a well in the centre and add the liquid glucose and 25ml (5 tsp) of the cold water. Begin to mix the paste; if it is too stiff, add a further 5ml (1 tsp) water. Continue mixing until all the ingredients are well blended. Transfer the paste to a clean work surface or board and knead in the pastello or sugarpaste thoroughly.
● Divide the paste into three or four portions and store in polythene bags in an airtight container in the refrigerator until required. This paste will keep for up to 2 – 3 months.
● If you require a coloured stencilling paste, substitute liquid food colouring for some of the water. It is a lot quicker and easier to make a deep shade using this method and also much cleaner than kneading in paste colouring once the paste is mixed.

ROYAL ICING

15ml (1 tbsp) albumen powder
75ml (2½ fl oz/⅓ cup) cold water
500g (1 lb/3 cups) icing (confectioners')
sugar, sifted

● Dissolve the albumen powder in the cold water and leave to stand for about 30 minutes, stirring occasionally. Put the sugar in a bowl and pour in the albumen mixture.
● Using an electric mixer on the slowest speed, mix for about 12 – 15 minutes, or until the icing reaches a soft piping consistency.

Making your own stencils can be quite a time-consuming process. It involves drawing a design or pattern, transferring it onto either acetate or polyester film and then cutting it out. An extensive range of pre-cut stencils specifically designed for cake decorating is now available from good sugarcraft supply shops. There are also stencils intended for interior decorating, but you may find some of the designs too large for cakes.

CHOOSING AND ADAPTING A SUBJECT

My inspiration comes from many sources. As well as working from my own drawings, greeting cards, books, photographs and so on also provide ideas. Simple line drawings can easily be adapted to use for stencil decoration. Flowers probably have the widest appeal for stencilling as they are so easily adapted. They can be drawn in their natural form or they can be stylized and arranged in a patterned border. There are many ways to vary a theme, but often the best approach is to sketch as many ideas as you can until you find the most suitable composition. The images can be increased or reduced in size on a photocopier to fit the appropriate space.

The examples below show how I have developed some ideas so that they can be applied as stencil decoration. The many variations that

can be introduced to these ideas include border designs and cake top decorations. Each idea is developed, arranged and rearranged in different ways. At this stage it is worth making sketches on paper and laying them on the cake to see whether they will work or whether they should be smaller or larger. This is a very important part of developing an idea as it is a waste of time cutting a stencil only to find it doesn't fit!

DRAWING AND CUTTING STENCILS

❖

A stencil is made from a network of lines, known as bridges. In order to understand how a line drawing is transferred into stencil form, remember that the black line in a drawing becomes the white line in a stencil. Obviously the more detailed the drawing, the more intricate the stencil. All bridges should ideally link to one another; however, there are some exceptions where they do not. Examples of this are shown in some of the projects in this book, for example on the Daffodil Cake, see page 20. Stencilled decoration can also be made working with two or more stencils, first one and then another, to add further detail, for example on the Stencilled Strawberries cake, see page 38.

When the drawing is prepared, lay a piece of stencil film on top and trace the image, using a waterproof pen. It sometimes helps to secure the film with a piece of masking tape. Place the stencil on a cutting mat to cut it out. When cutting straight lines in the design, always start cutting in one corner and continue to the next. When cutting around curves, avoid angular edges by keeping the blade in position and curving gently as you move and cut at the same time. This takes a little practice.

It is very important to spend time cutting the stencil, as any imperfections are exaggerated when applied to an iced surface. If a bridge is cut across by mistake, it can be repaired by sticking a small piece of adhesive tape over the damaged area and re-cutting. This is not always necessary – provided the stencil remains flat, it can be used without repairing. Wash the stencil after use with a soft brush and warm soapy water, rinse and dry flat.

~ 1 ~

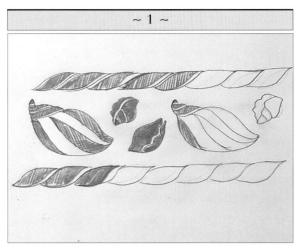

Before cutting your stencil, mark the areas that have to be cut away on a traced copy of the design. This is not essential, but it helps to show what should remain.

~ 2 ~

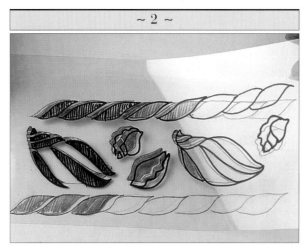

Trace the line drawing onto stencil film, using a waterproof pen.

~ 3 ~

Cut on either side of the drawn line, making sure that the cuts meet accurately on corners so that the pieces fall out. Never try to tug at these corners if they are caught as this may distort the stencil.

REGISTRATION MARKS

When building up a more complicated design with more than one stencil, registration marks should be drawn on each stencil. For example, when applying different colours which overlap, as on the Stencilled Strawberries, see page 67. Lay a rule across the centre of the design and draw a short line at the top and bottom, clear of the template. Then lay the rule in the opposite direction and draw lines horizontally clear of the sides of the design. Do this on each stencil. Check that the registration marks are correct before using the stencils by overlaying the top one in position. With registration marks, the exact position for the top template is easily found even when the bottom one is covered with colouring.

PREPARING TO USE YOUR STENCIL

❖

Knead a small amount of white vegetable fat (shortening) into a piece of stencilling paste. This is always necessary every time you prepare the paste for stencilling. Roll out the paste on a non-stick surface, large enough to cover the design on the stencil. The thickness of the paste depends on its use. For example, the paste should be thicker for a plaque. Some designs call for very finely rolled paste; the shapes on An Outrageous Birthday Cake, see page 42, and the kites on the Kite Cake, see page 14, have to be rolled thinly so that they do not look clumsy. For general purposes the paste is usually rolled out to 2.5 – 3mm (⅛ in) thick.

~ 1 ~

Prepare and roll out the paste. Lift the paste back over the rolling pin and place the stencil on the board. Lay the paste carefully on the stencil.

~ 2 ~

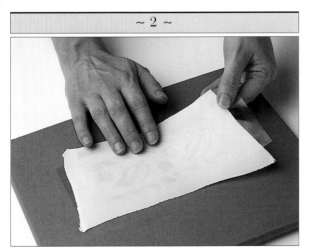

To secure the paste to the stencil, press down with the palm of your hand. Do not use a rolling pin as you would create a double image by rolling backwards and forwards.

~ 3 ~

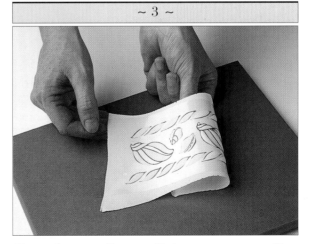

Turn the stencil over. Take care not to allow the paste to fall away from the stencil. If they do separate, it is better to roll up the paste and start again. The paste could be too dry, so add a little more white vegetable fat (shortening).

COLOURING TECHNIQUES

When dusting on colour, the moisture of the stencilling paste enables the dusting powder (petal dust/blossom tint) to stick. This surface will remain moist enough to apply colour for about 30 minutes. After this time it can still be applied but it is difficult to achieve depth of colour.

When applying colour, always work with the palest colours first. Deeper shades can be brushed over the top which helps to create depth. Working with the paler colours first also helps to prevent too many mistakes and overlapping colours. As the colour is applied, it should be left on the surface until all areas are coloured since any uncoloured exposed icing at this stage can be marked by loose dusting powder moving across the surface.

The shell border demonstrates the two different dusting techniques. When all the areas are dusted, remove all the loose dusting powder on the surface with a puffer and check the stencil to be sure that nothing has been missed, as once the stencil has been removed, it cannot be replaced.

EXPERT ADVICE

~

Avoid any creases and lumps in the stencilling paste as these will show up when dusting with colourings. Never coat the non-stick surface of stencil film with white vegetable fat (shortening) as this would make the icing too oily and cause marking throughout the stencil.

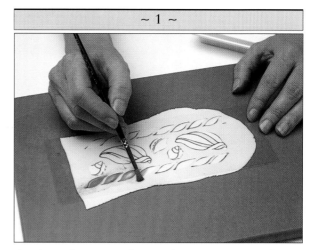

~ 1 ~

Apply colour to the surface, dusting off the stencil surface and onto the icing. To create a toning effect, use a sweeping brush stroke to apply the colour. White dusting powder can be added to the colour to soften the shades if necessary.

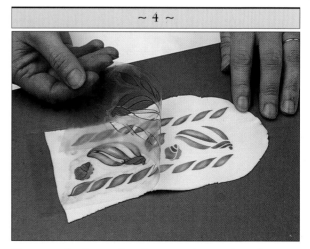

~ 4 ~

Remove the loose dusting powder and peel away the stencil.

~ 2 ~

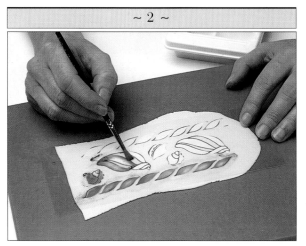

Brush a little more firmly to darken the edges. Avoid pale areas at the edge as they are less likely to stand out from the background if it is also pale.

~ 3 ~

Stipple the more detailed areas to ensure that the colour sticks on the surface. You may need to use a smaller brush.

~ 5 ~

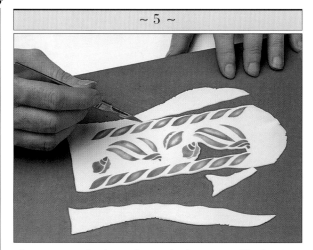

Cut around the edge of the stencilled piece carefully, leaving a narrow border all the way around. This needs to be a similar width to the bridges that run through the stencil.

EXPERT ADVICE

≈

Before you begin, lay out all the colours and brushes you will require. Clean your brush with cornflour (cornstarch) on a piece of absorbent kitchen paper. Only wash your brushes when you know that they will not be needed immediately. Keep a separate brush for black as it is impossible to clean properly.

KITE CAKE

*T*his delightful cake is a bright and colourful example of using a very simple stencil shape and is ideal if you are short of time. The lettering on the top has been made using a set of alphabet cutters. Alternatively, you can stencil the letters by using the alphabet templates on page 37.

18cm (7 in) square cake
185g (6 oz) buttercream
1kg (2 lb) white sugarpaste
125g (4 oz) Stencilling Paste, see page 6
white vegetable fat (shortening)
dusting powders (petal dusts/blossom tints):
daffodil yellow, fern green, poinsettia red
and violet
clear alcohol (gin or vodka)
small amount of Royal Icing, see page 6
E Q U I P M E N T
25cm (10 in) cake board
green tissue paper
spray glue
sticky-backed plastic
1m (1 yd 3 in) each of red, green and
yellow ribbon
alphabet cutters
stencil film
pieces of foam sponge

● Decorate the cake board with green tissue

EXPERT ADVICE

≈

If no alphabet cutters are available, the lettering can be piped in royal icing.

---

paper, sticking it down with spray glue, and cover with sticky-backed plastic to seal the surface.

● Cover the cake with buttercream and smooth over with a palette knife. Coat with white sugarpaste, smoothing the top and sides. Transfer the cake to the prepared cake board and trim with ribbon.

● Colour some small pieces of stencilling paste in the same shades as the ribbon and cut out the lettering. Arrange on top of the cake and secure with clear alcohol. Colour a selection of kites using the dusting powders in the order shown in the step-by-step photograph. Leave to dry.

● When all the pieces are completely dry, position them on the cake and secure with royal icing, angling the kites to create a floating effect. You may need to support them with small wedges of foam sponge until they are dry.

Begin by colouring the kites with yellow, then use green, red and violet. Stipple the dusting powder where the colours are adjacent to each other. Cut out each section carefully and leave to dry. The tails of the kites can be twisted slightly before drying.

VALENTINE'S CAKE

I have chosen to use a deep shade of rose red to enhance the contrast of colours used in the stencil. This design is quite intricate and I have only used part of it for this particular project. The whole design can be used either in the same way or it can be draped over the cake surface. The cake surface has been kept plain and the cake board decorated in a rather unusual way to complement it.

20cm (8 in) heart-shaped cake
1kg (2 lb) marzipan (almond paste)
clear alcohol (gin or vodka)
1kg (2 lb) sugarpaste
rose paste food colouring
185g (6 oz) Stencilling Paste, see page 6
white vegetable fat (shortening)
rose, poinsettia, cyclamen, nasturtium,
sunflower, leaf green, holly green, ivy green,
lilac and white dusting powders (petal
dusts/blossom tints) and airbrush colours
EQUIPMENT
13cm (5 in) heart-shaped thin card template
25cm (10 in) heart-shaped cake board
75 x 50cm (30 x 20 in) sheet of
white tissue paper
stencil film
airbrush
spray glue
20cm (8 in) greaseproof paper
(parchment) heart
craft knife
smoother
double-sided adhesive tape

● Make the stencilled plaque before covering the cake so that the paste is completely dry and can be inserted into the top of the freshly covered cake. This will enable you to fit the plaque in neatly by easing the sugarpaste close to the plaque. Using the heart-shaped card template, cut out the paste and transfer to another board. Leave to dry for 24 hours.

● Cover the cake board as described in the step-by-step instructions, see page 19, and prepare the surface for the cake by covering with a piece of greaseproof paper (parchment).

● Cover the cake with marzipan. Brush with clear alcohol, leaving the area for the central heart plaque dry. Then cover the cake with deep rose-coloured sugarpaste and remove the heart-shaped section ready to insert the plaque.

● When the cake has been decorated, transfer it to the prepared cake board and trim with the decorative paper ribbon. Make a bow from tissue paper, scrunching the paper lengthwise before tying it. Secure to the cake board with double-sided adhesive tape.

EXPERT ADVICE
≈

If you do not have an airbrush, sponge colour onto the stencil when decorating the board. Be careful not to wet the paper too much.

~ 1 ~

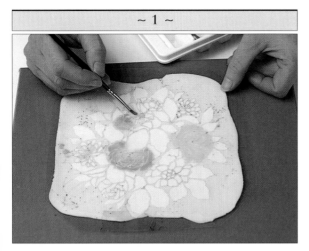

Roll out 185g (6 oz) stencilling paste 3mm (⅛ in) thick and large enough to cover the stencil design. Apply the paste to the stencil. Begin colouring using sunflower yellow to dust some of the chrysanthemums and lightly colour part of one of the roses. Use soft pink to over-dust the rose to create a two-tone effect.

~ 2 ~

Apply the other colours in the same way and finish by dusting the deepest shades. A touch of red or cyclamen on the leaves gives a lovely warm effect.

EXPERT ADVICE

≈

If the stencilled plaque does not fit exactly into the space on the cake top, the sugarpaste must be eased towards it evenly all the way around with your hand and a smoother, taking care not to distort the heart cut-out of the top of the cake when doing this. If the plaque is too big, be careful not to force it into the space on the cake as it may break. If it is too small, ease the sugarpaste around the edge to fill the gap. If it is difficult to close the gap, pipe a small snail trail border to neaten the join.

~ ❖ ~

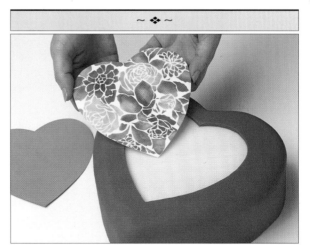

DECORATING THE CAKE Mask the cake top with the heart template, then brush the remaining marzipan with alcohol. Coat with rose-coloured sugarpaste. Replace the template, cut around it with a craft knife and lift out the paste. Immediately insert the stencilled plaque.

DECORATING THE BOARD

Lay a sheet of white tissue paper flat, shiny side up. Hold the stencil down firmly on the paper and spray using the airbrush. Decorate about half the sheet. When the colour is dry, follow the steps for cutting it and applying it to the board.

Secure the greaseproof paper (parchment) heart to the cake board with royal icing or apricot glaze. This is to prevent the coloured tissue paper coming into contact with cake. Position the cake on the cake board.

~ 1 ~

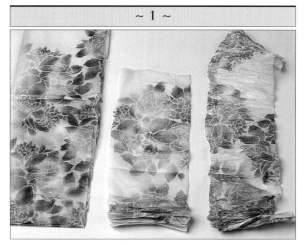

Cut the stencilled tissue into 10cm (4 in) wide strips. You should have about double the circumference of the board with enough left to make a bow. Scrunch up the paper tightly, twist it and stretch it out again.

~ 2 ~

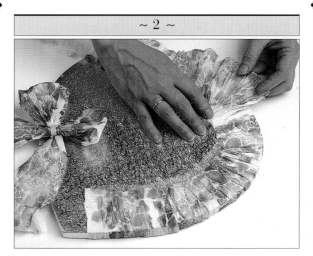

Spray the back of each strip generously with glue. Fit onto the board, gathering a little at a time. Cover the top edge with 5cm (2 in) overlap, then fold this down the sides and tuck the remainder underneath.

EXPERT ADVICE

≈

This stencil can really be coloured quite haphazardly, as overlapping colours will enhance the overall result. I actually encourage this when dusting this particular stencil.

DAFFODIL CAKE

*T*his is quite an unusual cake. Warm bright colours have been used to create a fresh spring-like appearance to correspond to the time of year for which it has been decorated. The sides have been decorated with a bold stripe and bow which displays the use of stencils in two rather different ways.

18cm (7 in) or 20cm (8 in) round cake
750g (1½ lb) marzipan (almond paste)
clear alcohol (gin or vodka)
2kg (4 lb) sugarpaste
daffodil, sunflower, marigold, berberis, nasturtium, chestnut, leaf green, holly and ivy green dusting powders (petal dusts/ blossom tints)
berberis, nasturtium and leaf green paste food colouring
315g (10 oz) Stencilling Paste, see page 6
white vegetable fat (shortening)
small amount of Royal Icing, see page 6

EQUIPMENT

25cm (10 in) or 28cm (11 in) cake board
coloured tissue paper
spray glue
sticky-backed plastic
craft knife
1cm (½ in) flat paintbrush
masking tape
stencil film
ruler
small piping bag
30 x 15cm (12 x 6 in) sheet fine graph paper
small block of foam sponge
tilt board (optional)

● Cover the cake board with orange tissue paper, attaching it with spray glue, and seal the surface with sticky-backed plastic.

● Cover the cake with marzipan. Brush with alcohol and coat with a thin layer of white sugarpaste. Leave to dry overnight.

● Lay a 13cm (5 in) diameter template on top of the cake and paint the remaining area with clear alcohol. Colour 750g (1½ lb) of the sugarpaste with deep berberis paste food colouring and use to coat the cake.

● Replace the 13cm (5 in) template as accurately as you can and cut around it with a sharp craft knife. Peel away the circle of berberis-coloured sugarpaste. Transfer to the covered cake board.

● Stencil the daffodil decoration using shades of yellows for the outer petals and oranges for the trumpets, then position it on the cake top following the step-by-step instructions on page 22.

● To complete the decoration, stencil the stripes. You will need to stencil three or four sections of paste to cover the side of the cake completely. The template for the stripes used on all cakes in this book is given on page 68.

● Finally, make the bow as described on page 19 and secure on the cake with royal icing.

EXPERT ADVICE

≈

An airbrush can be used to colour the stripes, using matching liquid food colourings.

COLOURING THE DAFFODIL STENCIL

❖

Follow the step-by-step instructions, taking great care when dusting the trumpets as some of the bridges are not linked at both ends. It is safer to stipple the colour in these areas to avoid the danger of lifting and damaging narrow areas of paste with the brush. When the colouring is completed, cut away all the excess white paste around the main body of the stencil and leave all pieces to dry separately before positioning them on the cake.

Begin by positioning the largest section on the cake as shown. Position and secure the trumpets in the same way, again applying more royal icing so that they sit even higher. They can also be positioned at an angle to accentuate the way in which they protrude.

MAKING THE STRIPE DECORATION

❖

The step-by-step instructions on page 24 show how to stencil stripes for any number of projects. When colouring paste which has to be applied to a cake while still soft, alcohol is mixed with the colour so that it dries quickly. This ensures that the pattern is dry, therefore it does not distort easily when the paste is used on the cake.

It is best to paint the narrow stripe first, in this case the nasturtium colour, and to work with small sections. Do not make the striped panel for the cake side too long as it will be difficult to handle.

This striped design is useful for concealing any blemishes on the basic sugarpaste covering on the cake.

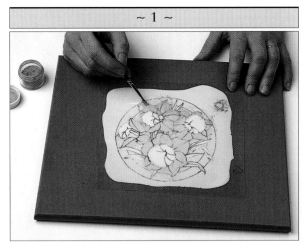

~ 1 ~

Begin by colouring the outside petals in daffodil and sunflower yellow. Brush over the top of some of the petals with marigold, a deeper yellow.

~ 4 ~

Cut out the trumpets of all the flowers, keeping the white border on the trumpet. Cut away some of the white background areas in between the flowers and stems. Always leave a thin white border to the stencilled sections. Leave to dry.

~ 2 ~

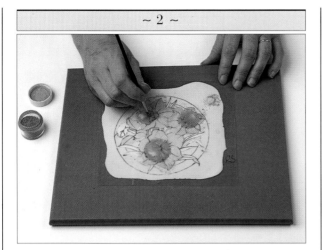

Colour the trumpets, shading carefully by using a lighter brush stroke to create a paler area in the throat of the trumpet. This will give more depth to the centre of the flowers. Stipple delicate bridges which are not linked at both ends.

~ 3 ~

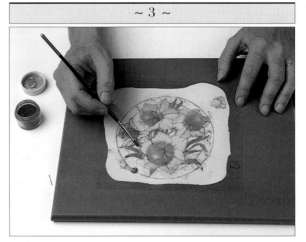

Colour the stems and leaves in leaf green, again overbrushing in the deeper holly and ivy green and chestnut. Remove all the excess dusting powder and clean up any areas that need attention.

~ 5 ~

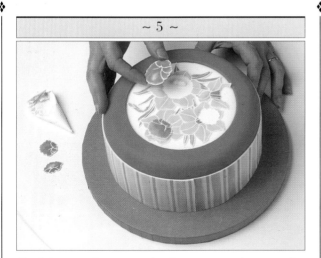

Position and secure the largest section on the cake with royal icing. Extra depth can be created by applying enough royal icing on the back so that the stencilled section does not lie flat on the surface.

USING INDIVIDUAL DAFFODILS

The daffodils in the stencil design may be traced and cut individually. As single flowers, they may be positioned on the corners of a cake, overlapping the top edge similar to collars. A border of single flowers around the edge of a round cake looks attractive. For an Easter celebration, continue the theme by decorating chocolate eggs with single daffodils to match the cake. The complete daffodil design can also be reduced on a photocopier and used to decorate the front of a sugar card, see Greeting Card on page 60.

~ 1 ~

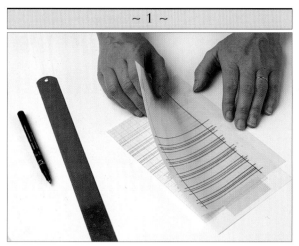

STRIPE DECORATION *Mark the required width of the stripes at regular intervals along top and bottom of the graph paper. Join the marks with lines. Lay stencil film on paper and secure both with masking tape. Use a fine pen and rule to trace stripes. Cut out the stripes in film.*

~ 2 ~

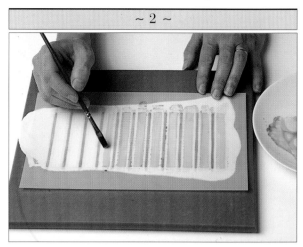

Mix the remaining white stencilling paste and sugarpaste together to make a weaker strength of stencilling paste. Apply the stencil to the paste in the usual way. Paint the stripes with paste food colouring thinned with alcohol, using nasturtium and leaf green alternately.

~ 3 ~

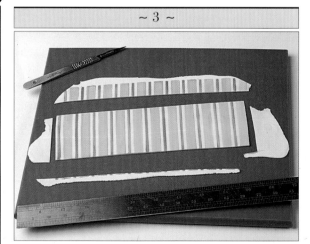

Before peeling off the stencil, move the paste to a board and leave to dry for 5 minutes before applying to the cake while making further striped sections. Measure and trim the top and bottom of the striped panel – usually 1cm (½ in) shorter than the cake depth.

~ 4 ~

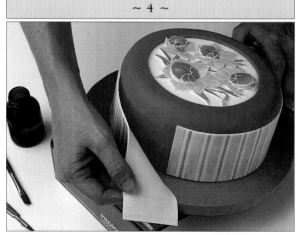

Place the cake on a tilt board or tilting turntable and paint the sides with alcohol. Transfer the striped sections carefully to the side of the cake and lay in position. When each section is fitted, make sure that the stripes match before applying the next.

STENCILLING WITH ROYAL ICING

*T*his cake shows a very simple example of stencilling with royal icing. A navy-coloured cake looks smart and helps to emphasize the white stencilled pattern. The decoration is done directly onto the cake, so there is no room for mistakes! Alternatively, the stencil can be used with dusting powders (petal dusts/blossom tints) or Baber colours and applied to a separate piece of stencilling paste. Baber colours are food colouring with an opaque, slightly milky appearance.

18cm (7 in) square cake
750g (1½ lb) marzipan (almond paste)
clear alcohol (gin or vodka)
1kg (2 lb) sugarpaste
wisteria blue paste food colouring
250g (8 oz) Royal Icing, see page 6
white vegetable fat (shortening)
EQUIPMENT
25cm (10 in) square cake board
white tissue paper
stencil film
tilt board
steel icing rule
adhesive tape
3mm (⅛ in) wide white ribbon to trim cake

● Decorate the board with pleated tissue paper, following the step-by-step instructions on page 26.
● Cover the cake with marzipan. Brush with alcohol and coat the cake with navy-coloured sugarpaste. Leave to dry overnight. The sugarpaste must be dry before applying the stencil as it is very easy to dent the soft paste

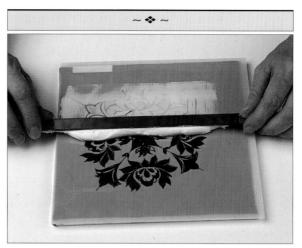

Ask an assistant to hold the stencil firmly in place. Apply the icing to the edge of a steel rule, lay at one edge of the design and carefully pull across the surface. Do not stop until you reach the end. If there are any areas that have been missed, repeat this process before moving the stencil.

when holding the stencil in position.
● Using a slightly thicker stencil film, make the stencil as shown on page 9 and using the templates on page 65. A thicker film will give more relief to the royal icing but it is a little more difficult to cut. The royal icing should be a slightly softer consistency to that used when covering a cake.
● Stencil the top of the cake following the step-by-step instructions. Lay the side stencil in position and use a palette knife to apply royal icing to the sides.
● Secure narrow white ribbon on the sides of the cake, around the bottom edge and towards the top edge. Alternatively, thin white lines can either be incorporated in the stencil design or piped on with royal icing. A bow of ribbon may be added, if liked.

COVERING THE CAKE BOARD

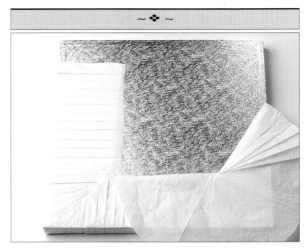

Cut a 50 x 10cm (20 x 4 in) strip of white tissue paper and pleat it into 1cm (½ in) folds. The finished piece should measure 15cm (6 in). Repeat this process a further three times. Cut a 23cm (9 in) diameter circle of tissue paper and cut a slim wedge out of the circle. Pleat the circle of paper from the centre outwards, so that you have a wedge of pleated paper, about a quarter of the size of the original circle. Repeat this process three times so that there are four pleated quarters of a circle.

Secure the paper to the cake board with adhesive tape, beginning with a section on one side of the board. Continue around the board, pleating the paper neatly on the corners. Make sure that the final overlap lies correctly.

When the outer area of the board is neatly covered with the strips of paper, cover the central area with the four quarters to make a complete circle. This will hold the paper securely in place.

Covering the board with pleated tissue paper. The paper is applied in sections, starting at one side of the board and applying pleated strips all around, then fixing four quarters of a circle to neaten the centre of the board.

Side Decoration

PORTRAIT CAKE

*T*his cake was designed with a view to framing and keeping the plaque. It takes time and care to produce something that is near to a photograph. I had to omit the cardigan on the little girl because it was too difficult to stencil; this artistic licence is important for successful composition.

23 x 18cm (9 x 7 in) oval cake
1kg (2 lb) marzipan (almond paste)
clear alcohol (gin or vodka)
1kg (2 lb) white sugarpaste
bluegrass, mint, fern and bulrush paste food colourings
flesh, chestnut, poinsettia, wisteria, bluegrass, white, berberis, marigold and bulrush dusting powders (petal dusts/blossom tints)
100g (3 oz) Stencilling Paste, see page 6
white vegetable fat (shortening)
E Q U I P M E N T
30 x 25cm (12 x 10 in) oval cake board
stencil film
tissue paper
double-sided adhesive tape
soft cotton cloth for ragging
craft knife
selection of wide paintbrushes
25 x 20cm (10 x 8 in) oval cake card, optional
spray glue

● Following the instructions on page 30, make the stencilled plaque in advance so that it is ready to insert into the top of the cake. It is also better to have decorated the cake board at this stage so that the cake can be easily transferred to it when complete, see right.
● Cover the cake with marzipan. Mask the area

for the plaque, moisten with clear alcohol and coat with white sugarpaste. Then remove the oval section ready to insert the plaque. This technique is shown on page 18.
● Rag the surface of the cake with a thin mixture of paste colour and alcohol, then transfer the cake to the prepared board.
● Make a bow from the remaining piece of matching tissue paper, and secure to the cake board with double-sided adhesive tape.

RAGGING THE CAKE SURFACE

❖

The illustration shows the effect which should be achieved when ragging. Always remember to test the colour on a sheet of paper before applying it to the cake.

Mix a thin solution of bluegrass paste food colouring and alcohol. Moisten the cotton cloth with water and dip into the colour mixture. Scrunch the cloth up loosely and lightly rag the cake, avoiding the plaque on the top. Here the technique is shown on a plain sugarpaste-covered board.

MAKING THE STENCIL

Trace the photograph, taking particular care around the face. Do not trace clothing detail, such as stripes on socks. Cut the stencil, face first, as if mistakes are made it can quickly be discarded without having wasted too much time.

EXPERT ADVICE

≈

When cutting the stencil, it is important to cut exactly as drawn around the face, arms and legs. It is not quite as critical if you happen to waver off the line when cutting around the clothing. Study the photograph in detail for the colouring, particularly on the flesh tones.

~ 2 ~

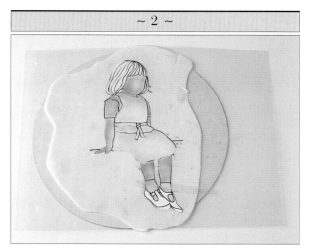

Stencil the figure as usual, starting with the flesh tones, adding soft hints of pink and brown to build up depth of colour and shadow. Take care not to apply too much colour. Then colour darker areas, such as hair. Shade the dress in pale bluegrass; colour the shoes blue and red.

~ 3 ~

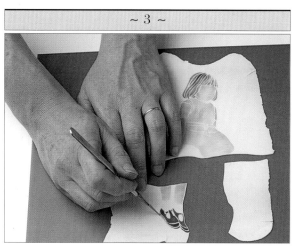

Using a craft knife, cut off the head and legs of the figure before cutting away the excess paste.

~ 4 ~

Trace the face onto the stencilled image from the photograph and paint the line detail, using a very fine paintbrush and brown paste food colouring mixed with alcohol.

~ 5 ~

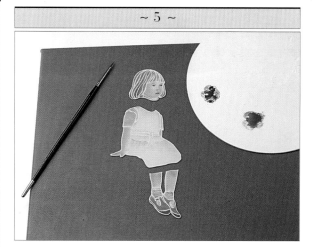

Fill in the eyes and lips, using a thin mixture of paste food colouring and alcohol. Paint further detail to the dress and shoes.

ASSEMBLING THE STENCILLED PIECES ON THE PLAQUE

❖

The pieces of the stencil should be left to dry before they can be assembled on the plaque. The background is painted before the figure is attached to the plaque.

EXPERT ADVICE

≈

The stencilled plaque has been placed on a thin cake card to give extra body. This helps to prevent dampness seeping into it from the moisture of the cake. It is also easier to remove before the cake is cut. The picture can then be mounted in a deep frame and kept indefinitely, providing it is kept out of direct sunlight.

It is also possible to paint portraits on sugar using an airbrush, but this takes a lot of practice to achieve colour control.

Prepare the background on an oval plaque. Mix a very weak solution of bluegrass paste food colouring with alcohol and paint a vertical wash, using a wide paintbrush. Paint further detail, using similar pale tones, to indicate the wall and the greenery.

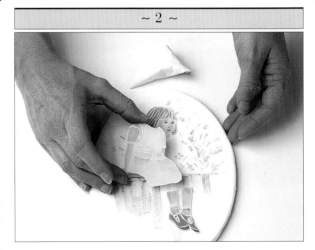

When the plaque is dry, assemble the figure. Secure each piece with a small amount of royal icing. Begin with the head and legs, followed by the main part of the body.

CHILD'S BIRTHDAY CAKE

*T*his very colourful cake is ideal for a child's birthday celebration. The inscription has been stencilled using a round-shaped lettering, see page 37, to complement the clouds that are floating onto the top of the cake. It is a relatively simple and quick cake to make although special care must be taken when cutting the stencil. The train stencil has also been adapted to make a greeting card in sugar. This stencil can also be used to decorate napkin rings and place setting cards.

20 x 15cm (8 x 6 in) cake
185g (6 oz) buttercream
1.5kg (3 lb) sugarpaste
clear alcohol (gin or vodka)
poinsettia red or Christmas red paste food colouring
poinsettia red, mint, sunflower, bulrush, gentian and black dusting powders (petal dusts/blossom tints)
icing (confectioners') sugar to dust
250g (8 oz) Stencilling Paste, see page 6
white vegetable fat (shortening)
small amount of Royal Icing, see page 6

E Q U I P M E N T
25 x 20cm (10 x 8 in) cake board
paper to cover the cake board
sticky-backed plastic
white card
craft knife
tilt board
glass-headed pins
candles (optional)

● Cover the cake board with paper and seal the surface with sticky-backed plastic. Cover the cake with a thin layer of buttercream, smoothing it over with a palette knife, and coat with white sugarpaste, smoothing the top and sides. Transfer the cake to the prepared cake board. Leave to dry overnight.

● Colour the remaining sugarpaste red. Remember that you can also buy a coloured paste to save time. Using a sharp knife, score two lines horizontally all the way around the cake 1cm (½ in) and 5cm (2 in) from the base. Paint clear alcohol over the surface of the cake avoiding the area between the two score lines around the sides.

● Roll out the red sugarpaste. Before laying it over the cake, sprinkle extra icing sugar underneath to help to prevent the red paste marking the band of white sugarpaste that is shortly to be exposed. Cover the cake in the usual way. Cut the same horizontal lines as before around the cake into the red paste and peel away a band all around the sides.

● Decorate the cake with the stencilled pieces. Finally, secure the name or greeting on the cake with a small amount of royal icing. Decorate the cake with the appropriate number of candles if liked.

EXPERT ADVICE

≈

If you don't have an airbrush, the sky can be painted by hand. This idea can be used to decorate a cake in the same way.

~ 1 ~

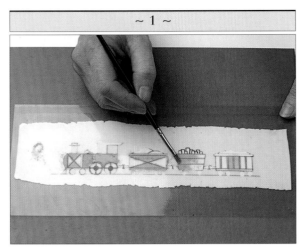

Begin by colouring the yellows and greens. Stipple the colour very firmly on the surface to get a brighter, more vibrant finish.

~ 2 ~

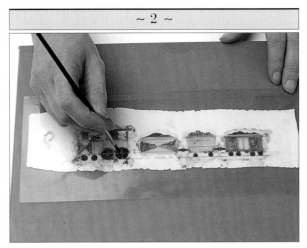

Continue colouring the train, working through the colours in order of paler or brighter shades first. Finally, dust the black on, using a tiny movement as you stipple the colour on the surface to avoid overlapping.

~ 3 ~

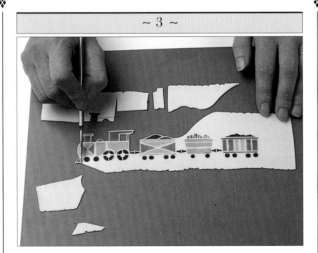

Remove all the loose dusting powder and clean away any areas where the colour has overlapped. Peel away the stencil and cut off the excess paste.

~ 4 ~

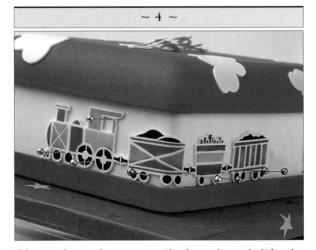

Place the cake on a tilt board and lift the stencilled train carefully into position. Bend one of the trailers so that it goes around the corner. Do not secure to the cake yet, just pin in position until dry. Secure with a small amount of royal icing.

CUTTING OUT THE CLOUDS AND STENCILLING THE NAME

❖

Trace the cloud templates onto card, see below. Roll out a sheet of white stencilling paste and use the templates below to cut out several cloud shapes.

Apply the stencilling paste to the name or greeting in the usual way, but remember to lay the stencil on the board back to front, so that when it is turned over to dust it will read correctly. Peel away the stencil and cut out with a craft knife, keeping the letters linked together as shown in the photograph of the finished cake.

> **EXPERT ADVICE**
>
> ≈
>
> Do not colour all the sections of the train the same way, change the order in which the colours are applied without altering the selection of colours.

GREETING CARD

❖

200g (6½ oz) Stencilling Paste, see page 6
small amount of gum tragacanth
small amount of Royal Icing, see page 6
gentian, mint, poinsettia red, sunflower, black and bulrush liquid food colouring and dusting powders (petal dusts/blossom tints)
clear alcohol (gin or vodka)
EQUIPMENT
airbrush
steel rule
piping bag
plain writing piping tube (tip)
small blossom plunger cutter

● Knead a small amount of gum tragacanth into the stencilling paste so that it dries very firmly. Roll out and cut out the card as shown in the step-by-step illustrations.

● Decorate the background of the card using an airbrush and use the appliqué method to decorate the foreground, securing the train to the card with clear alcohol. Leave to dry completely.

● To assemble the card, pipe a line of royal icing along the top of the back of the card and fix the front on at an angle of about 45 degrees.

~ 1 ~

Roll out a sheet of stencilling paste, about 3mm (⅛ in) thick. Cut out two 20 x 8cm (8 x 3½ in) pieces. Lay the cloud templates on one section and airbrush the sky blue. Remove the templates.

~ 2 ~

Roll out a small piece of green stencilling paste to cover the width of the card. Cut a wavy cut along the top and trim the bottom and sides to fit the card. Secure with clear alcohol. Colour the train, see page 34, cut and gently bend to fit on the top of the green paste. Secure with clear alcohol. Trim with plunger cutter flowers.

STENCILLED STRAWBERRIES

*T*his cake demonstrates the use of stencil designs that are coloured in two stages, using two different stencils to add further detail to the strawberries and leaves. The cake is covered with two layers of sugarpaste, exposing the lighter layer underneath so that the stencilled pieces overhang this area to create depth in the design. The cake board has been decorated by painting the sugarpaste surface before using as a wrapping.

18cm (7 in) square cake
750g (1½ lb) marzipan (almond paste)
clear alcohol (gin or vodka)
2kg (4 lb) sugarpaste
140g (4½ oz) Stencilling Paste, see page 6
white vegetable fat (shortening)
leaf green and poinsettia red paste
food colourings
leaf green, poinsettia red, chestnut, black
and white dusting powders (petal dusts/
blossom tints)
small amount of Royal Icing, see page 6
piping gel

EQUIPMENT

25cm (10 in) square cake board
1cm (½ in) wide paintbrush
13cm (5 in) diameter round card template
craft knife
piping bag
two no. 0 piping tubes (tips)
pieces of foam sponge
stencil film
masking tape
black and red waterproof pens
red ribbon to trim cake

● Decorate the cake board as described on page 40 and leave to dry for a couple of days before the cake is placed on it. Cover the cake with marzipan. Brush with clear alcohol and coat with a thin layer of white sugarpaste. Leave to dry for a couple of days.

● Place the card template in the centre of the cake to mask this area and paint the remaining area with clear alcohol. Remove the template and cover the cake with pale leaf green-coloured sugarpaste. Replace the card template as accurately as you can in the centre of the cake and cut around it with a craft knife. Peel back this section carefully and discard it.

● Pipe the border of royal icing beads inside the circle before attaching the stencilled sections. Use two piping bags fitted with no. 0 piping tubes (tips): one filled with red royal

---

EXPERT ADVICE

≈

A small amount of stencilling paste can be mixed with the sugarpaste to give it a little more body. Use a steel rule to keep the lines straight and measure an equal distance of about 2.5cm (1 in) between the stripes. The colour will dry fairly rapidly because it has been mixed with alcohol. However, the surface may need to be dusted lightly with icing (confectioners') sugar or cornflour (cornstarch) if it is still tacky before applying to the cake board. It is easier to hold the cake board on the palm of one hand while wrapping the paste around it with the other. If the overhang is too heavy, trim off a little as it may be inclined to tear with too much weight.

icing, the other with white. Pipe alternate beads of red and white. A greeting can also be written in the centre of the cake at this stage.

• Follow the step-by-step instructions to make the stencil decoration. Registration marks have to be drawn on the stencils to align one stencil on top of another so that the stems and veins are positioned correctly. It is important that the detail on the second stencil is accurately cut so that it can be placed exactly over the detail of the first one. Repeat this process to make the smaller strawberry stencil, again drawing registration marks on both parts 1 and 2. Cut the stencils by following the instructions below.

• As each stencilled section is made, it can be positioned and secured on the cake with clear alcohol and supported with pieces of foam sponge wherever extra lift is required.

• This stencil can be dried flat and applied to the cake top for a part-collar effect.

MAKING AND USING THE STENCILS

❖

The design consists of two stencils: the first drawn in black is an outline of fruit and leaves, the second drawn in red adds the detail. Follow the step-by-step instructions for tracing and applying the stencils.

EXPERT ADVICE
≈

If you are short of time, the stencil can be coloured, trimmed and left in one piece. The petals and leaves can be lifted and dried without detaching from the main body of the stencil.

~ 1 ~

Secure the stencil film over the strawberry drawing with masking tape. Trace the outline of the strawberries and leaves in black pen. Mark the registration points as indicated. Make a second stencil in red for the detail; remember the registration marks.

When the design is complete, cut around the stencilled piece carefully, leaving a thin white border. Position and secure on the cake with clear alcohol, lifting some of the strawberries and leaves and supporting them with pieces of foam sponge until dry.

DECORATING THE CAKE BOARD

❖

Roll out 500g (1 lb) white sugarpaste on a large non-stick board, large enough to cover the cake board, plus extra to tuck underneath the board. Mix 20 – 25ml (4 – 5 tsp) clear alcohol with poinsettia red paste food colouring. Paint 1cm (½ in) wide stripes on the sugarpaste.

Turn the board 90 degrees and paint the same width stripes again, creating a chequered effect. Use the painted sugarpaste to cover the board as shown in the step-by-step instructions.

~ 2 ~

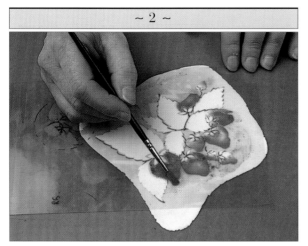

Apply 30g (1 oz) stencilling paste to the stencil as usual. Dust with poinsettia red dusting powder, making some of the strawberries a deeper shade than others.

~ 3 ~

Colour the leaves and overdust the strawberries in leaf green, then tip some of the leaves in red. Remove all the loose dusting powder and peel away the stencil.

~ 4 ~

Place the second stencil on top immediately: the moisture of the white areas should help it to adhere to the surface. Hold the stencil firmly in place and stipple the white and black areas. Remove the loose dusting powder and then the stencil.

~ 5 ~

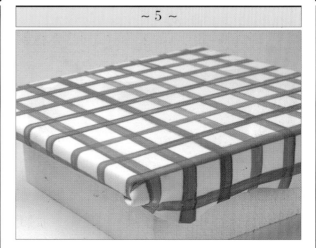

Paint the cake board with piping gel and wrap the chequered sheet of sugarpaste over the top, around the sides and underneath, securing the folds with piping gel.

AN OUTRAGEOUS BIRTHDAY CAKE

*T*he combination of the airbrushing and stencil dusting in 3-D is rather unusual and exciting. This cake would be ideal for a teenager who, perhaps, fits in with the wild and energetic decoration!

20cm (8 in) round cake
1kg (2 lb) marzipan (almond paste)
clear alcohol (gin or vodka)
1kg (2 lb) white sugarpaste
100g (3½ oz) Stencilling Paste, see page 6
white vegetable fat (shortening)
poinsettia, sunflower, hydrangea, mint and cyclamen liquid food colourings and dusting powders (petal dusts/blossom tints)
icing (confectioners') sugar
small amount of Royal Icing, see page 6

EQUIPMENT
28cm (11 in) cake board
white paper
sticky-backed plastic
two large sheets of stencil film (A3)
adhesive tape
airbrush
glass-headed pins
sponge foam pieces

● Cover the cake board with a layer of white paper and sticky-backed plastic before decorating the cake. Cover the cake with marzipan and leave to dry.

● Make the stencils as shown on page 71. If your stencil film is A4 size sheets, join them with adhesive tape, avoiding an overlap. Make the first pattern sheet as shown on page 44.

● Roll out the sugarpaste on a large non-stick surface. Apply the paste to the stencil in the usual manner. This will be a little more difficult to do as the sugarpaste will stretch when lifted. Turn over the sugarpaste and stencil and airbrush the colours. Change colour as you work.

● Once the first sheet is complete, remove and lay the second sheet on top immediately. It will not stick quite as well as the first as it cannot be applied in the same way. However, the white background should still be slightly tacky. This will help but the second stencil should be held in place as you work. Spray on further colour.

● Repeat this process as many times as you like, overlapping some of the shapes each time to create the geometric pattern.

EXPERT ADVICE
≈

With a little practice it is possible to airbrush patterns within each shape. Cover the cake in the usual way. Handle the sugarpaste carefully in order to avoid too much distortion. Trim away the excess and place on the prepared cake board. Make a selection of dusted stencil pieces using the co-ordinating colours and leave to dry before securing on the cake with royal icing. Glass-headed pins may be needed to support some of the shapes until dry.

AIRBRUSHING THE STENCIL

❖

Follow the step-by-step illustrations for building up the pattern. The design can be overlapped as many times as you like, but don't forget that the surface of the icing will gradually dry out, therefore making it more difficult to stick the stencil down on the paste. Hold the stencil firmly in place as you build up the layers.

Make a selection of stencilled shapes, then cut them out and leave to dry. Arrange the shapes haphazardly on the cake and secure them with a small amount of royal icing.

If you do not have an airbrush, but would like to make this cake, stencil all the decoration with dusting powders (petal dusts/blossom tints), cut them out and stick on the sugarpaste-covered cake.

This design would also look stunning using black for the background and decorating with lustre colours.

~ 1 ~

Apply the stencil in the usual way and begin to colour with yellow and green, overlapping colours. Introduce a third colour at this stage if you like.

EXPERT ADVICE

≈

There are other ways this stencil can be used; for example, a section of it can be wrapped around a cake as a border design. It can be applied in a similar way to the Unusual Christmas Cake, see page 55, and if used on a very thin layer of stencilling paste, it can be draped over the surface of a cake to create a fabric effect.

~ 2 ~

Lay the second stencil on the paste, over the top of the first colours. Continue airbrushing with different colours

~ 3 ~

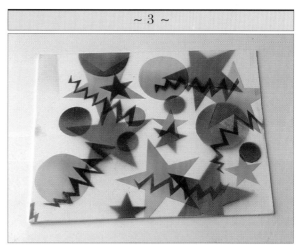

Continue to build up the pattern by laying the stencils on the paste, overlapping the previous colours and airbrushing with different colours.

~ 4 ~

Moisten the cake with clear alcohol and cover with the decorated sheet of sugarpaste. Trim away the excess.

~ 5 ~

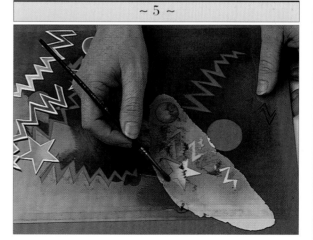

Make a selection of dusted stencil pieces, cut out and leave to dry thoroughly. Some of them can be shaped and curved before drying.

TIERED WEDDING CAKE

*T*his cake has been tiered in the conventional way and flowers have been arranged uniformly at the four corners of each cake. However, to escape from conventionality I have chosen to pattern part of the cake surface. The flowers are stylized and simple to make, and can be arranged easily on the cake. The cake has a 'front' as I decided to trim each tier with a matching bow. The colour theme remains the same throughout the decoration and is continued on the cake boards. The cakes have been tiered with perspex separators to retain a fresh summer mood.

*13cm (5 in), 18cm (7 in) and 23cm (9 in)
square cakes
2.5kg (5 lb) marzipan (almond paste)
4kg (8 lb) sugarpaste
clear alcohol (gin or vodka)
750g (1½ lb) Stencilling Paste, see page 6
white vegetable fat (shortening)
poinsettia red and leaf green liquid food
colourings
poinsettia red, sunflower, leaf green, hyacinth
and white dusting powders (petal dusts/
blossom tints)
small amount of Royal Icing, see page 6*

EXPERT ADVICE

≈

If you do not have an airbrush, paint the stripes by hand. Follow the instructions for painting the board covering on the Stencilled Strawberries, see page 38.

EQUIPMENT
*18cm (7 in), 23cm (9 in) and 28 cm (11 in)
square cake boards
green tissue paper
sticky-backed plastic
graph paper
two large sheets of stencil film (A3)
straight frill cutter
steel rule
airbrush
former
glass-headed pins
pieces of foam sponge*

● Decorate the cake boards with green tissue paper and seal the surface with sticky-backed plastic. Cover the cake with marzipan. Brush with clear alcohol and coat with a thin layer of white sugarpaste. Transfer the cakes to the prepared cake boards.

● Make the two different striped stencils using the graph paper so that they are as accurate as possible, the first sheet having the wider stripes and the second having the narrow stripes, see page 48.

● Divide the stencilling paste into 250g (8 oz) and 500g (1 lb) portions and mix the larger portion with the remaining white sugarpaste. Use this to decorate the top of each cake following the instructions on page 48 to apply the chequered effect. Fit the patterned sheet as neatly as possible. Make an extra sheet of chequered paste for the bows. Trim the edge of the chequered paste with a narrow, pale leaf-green frill.

● Arrange and secure the flowers on all three tiers. Attach the bows with royal icing to complete the decoration.

~ 1 ~

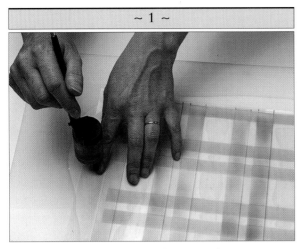

Roll the mixed stencilling and sugarpaste larger than the bottom tier. Apply the stencil and spray the stripes pink using a mixture of red liquid colouring and alcohol. Release the stencil and turn it by 90 degrees. Spray the stripes again. Remove the stencil.

~ 2 ~

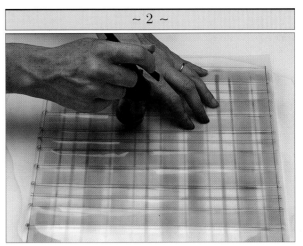

Position the second stencil: the damp paste will help to hold the stencil in place. Spray every fourth, wide, stripe pink. Then spray the remaining stripes in green. Release the stencil and turn it by 90 degrees. Spray the pink and green again to complete the chequered pattern.

~ 4 ~

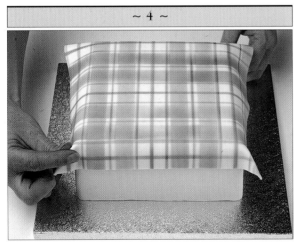

Ease the sheet down the top edge. Moisten the corners of the paste with clear alcohol and gently pinch them together to make neat pleats.

~ 5 ~

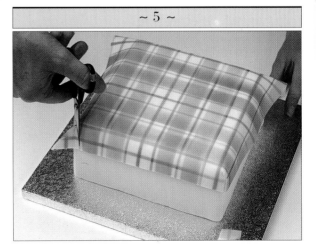

Cut off the pleats on the corners using small sharp scissors. Trim the overhang and secure with alcohol.

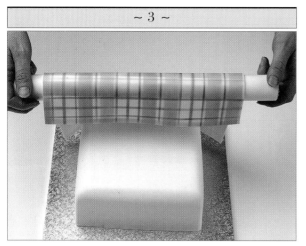

~ 3 ~

Moisten the top of the cake with clear alcohol. Lift the decorated sheet carefully over a rolling pin and position on the cake, lining up the pattern with the side of the cake.

~ 6 ~

Roll out pale green paste and cut out a thin lace section. Trim the edge of the chequered paste with this: do not moisten the paste too much as it will cause the lace to slip off.

ARRANGING THE FLOWERS AND LEAVES

Dry some of the flowers on a former, so that they set in a curved shape as shown in the step-by-step instructions. Stick some flowers directly onto the cake.

When all the pieces are dry, continue to add to the corner arrangements. The flowers may need to be supported with glass-headed pins until the royal icing with which they are attached is dry.

MAKING THE BOWS

Cut a 20 x 5cm (8 x 2 in) piece of chequered paste. Turn it upside down, paint the underneath with clear alcohol and fold both sides into the centre.

Fold the ends of the strip into the middle to make the loops of the bow and secure them with alcohol. Cut a small band of chequered paste and wrap it around the middle of the bow to conceal the join. Support the loops with pieces of foam sponge until they are dry.

This bow will be large enough for the bottom tier of the cake; make slightly smaller bows for the middle and top tiers, in proportion to the cakes. Secure the bows to the cakes with royal icing.

~ 1 ~

ARRANGING THE FLOWERS AND LEAVES *Make a selection of flowers and leaves. Dust just around the centre of the flowers first with a touch of yellow before colouring the centre green.*

~ 2 ~

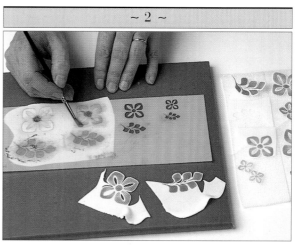

Dust the remaining part of the flower in pink. Colour all the leaves in shades of green. Cut out all the leaves and flowers, removing the solid white areas but always leaving a thin white border to the stencil.

~ ❖ ~

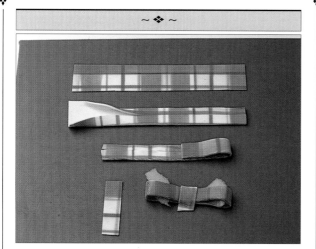

MAKING THE BOWS *The stages in making the bows, from cutting the strip of chequered paste, through folding and securing it in place, to supporting the loops with foam sponge until they are thoroughly dry.*

Leaf and Flower

BUMBLE BEES AND DAISIES

I thought it would be fun to combine airbrush work with a royal-iced stencil decoration. This has created a relief effect using the white royal icing for the daisy heads. The same combination has been used on top to make the bumble bees. These were made on a piece of stencilling paste, cut out and dried before placing on the cake.

18cm (7 in) round cake
1kg (2 lb) marzipan (almond paste)
clear alcohol (gin or vodka)
1kg (2 lb) sugarpaste
vine and marigold paste food colourings
mint and black liquid food colourings
small amount of Royal Icing, see page 6
small amount of Stencilling Paste,
see page 6
white vegetable fat (shortening)
EQUIPMENT
28cm (11 in) round cake board
green tissue paper
sticky-backed plastic
stencil film
piping bag
no. 0 piping tube (tip)
2m (2¼ yd) narrow black ribbon
airbrush
small pointed palette knife
craft knife
glass-headed pins

● Cover the cake board with green tissue paper and sticky-backed plastic. Cover the cake with marzipan. Brush with clear alcohol and coat with pale vine-coloured sugarpaste. Place on the prepared board. Leave to dry for a couple of days to avoid denting the surface during the next stage of the decoration.

● Cut out the stencils for the side decoration, see pages 66 and 68, and apply to the cake as shown on page 52, beginning by airbrushing the leaves, then adding the royal icing daisies. Use marigold-coloured royal icing and a no. 0 piping tube (tip) to pipe the rows of dots which make up the centres of the flowers.

● Stencil the bumble bees on the cake top, see page 54, and also make individual bees in stencilling paste. Leave to dry and stick onto the cake with royal icing, supporting the wings on pieces of foam sponge until the icing has dried.

● Pipe the finishing touches on the cake. Trim the bottom of the cake and the board with ribbon.

EXPERT ADVICE

≈

A third stencil could be made for the daisy heads instead of piping them on. While the stencil is still in place, and the icing wet, stick a little pollen dust to the surface to create a textured finish.

~ 1 ~

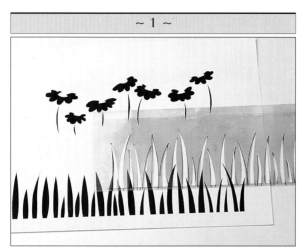

Cut out two stencils for the design on the side of the cake: the first includes the leaves, the second is for the flowers and stems.

~ 2 ~

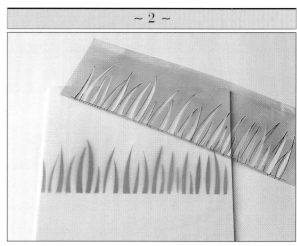

Hold the leaf stencil against the side of the cake with one hand and airbrush in mint green. Repeat all the way around the cake and remove the stencil.

~ 3 ~

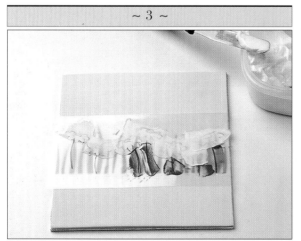

Stencil the daisy heads, scraping white royal icing across the stencil. Before taking the stencil away, scrape green royal icing across the daisy stems. Take care not to move the stencil at any time as you work.

MAKING THE 3-D BUMBLE BEES

❖

Follow the step-by-step instructions for stencilling the bees, applying the design to a thin sheet of soft stencilling paste. Cut around them with a craft knife, leaving a narrow white border as usual. Support the wings on pieces of foam sponge so that they dry in a slightly raised position.

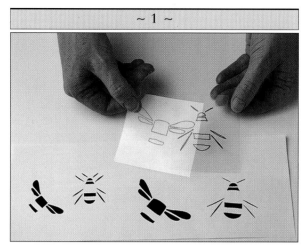

~ 1 ~

Cut the stencil in two parts, so that the black stripes and the legs are coloured in one stencil and the wings and yellow stripes are together in the other stencil.

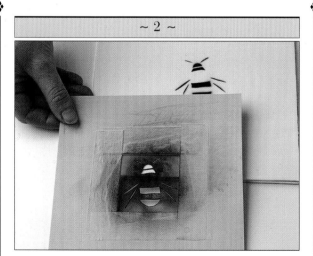

~ 2 ~

Position the first stencil on the cake. Mask off the surrounding area. Hold the stencil down firmly and airbrush the first section in black. Remove the stencil.

~ 3 ~

Position the second stencil on top as accurately as you can. Apply the marigold-coloured royal icing with a small pointed palette knife, avoiding the wings. Stencil the wings in white, working from the centres to the tips. Remove the stencil. Repeat for all the bees.

UNUSUAL CHRISTMAS CAKE

This cake was a pleasure to design and decorate. A simple theme of holly and berries runs throughout the decoration and the design is easily executed once all the stencils are cut. The large stencil pattern took about 6 hours to cut – because it was so repetitive, it was particularly tiring and was not cut in one session. The berries have to be very carefully cut to ensure they are round, not square!

18cm (7 in) round cake
1kg (2 lb) marzipan (almond paste)
clear alcohol (gin or vodka)
1kg (2 lb) cream sugarpaste
200g (7 oz) Stencilling Paste, see page 6
white vegetable fat (shortening)
poinsettia red, leaf green, dark gold and
berberis or cream liquid food colourings and
dusting powders (petal dusts/blossom tints)
icing (confectioners') sugar
small amount of Royal Icing, see page 6

EQUIPMENT
25cm (10 in) round cake board
large sheets of stencil film (A3)
airbrush
large ring cutter or card template
glass-headed pins
Garrett frill cutter

● Cover the cake with marzipan. Brush with clear alcohol and coat with cream-coloured sugarpaste. Leave to dry.

● Place on the prepared cake board. Measure the side of the cake and cut out a template. Divide it into equal sections and make an arched card template for cutting the scallops around the patterned paste. Use a round cutter or template to mark the centre of the cake top – this area must not be dampened with alcohol before applying the decorated paste.

● If you have only small sheets of stencil film (A4), join two sheets with adhesive tape avoiding an overlap. The template for the design is on page 69. Apply the first pattern sheet as shown on page 56. Roll out pale leaf-green sugarpaste on a large non-stick surface. Attach the stencil in the usual way. This will be a little more difficult to do as the sugarpaste will stretch when lifted. Turn over the sugarpaste and stencil, then airbrush the colours, changing colour as you work. As soon as the sheet is complete, remove the stencil, brush the cake top with clear alcohol, leaving the central circle and side dry, and lay the paste over the cake immediately. Handle the sugarpaste carefully in order to avoid too much distortion.

● Cut out the centre of the patterned paste and cut the scallops around the side as shown in the step-by-step instructions. Cut out frills in paste dusted with gold for trimming the circle in the middle of the cake and the scalloped edge.

● Make four dusted wreath stencil pieces using the pattern on page 69, cut out and leave to dry thoroughly. Make extra bows to use for trimming. Position and secure a wreath below alternate scallops on the cake side, attaching them with a small amount of royal icing on the back of each wreath. Pin to the side of the cake until dry. Attach bows under the scallops which are not decorated with wreaths. Place a wreath in the centre of the cake.

~ 1 ~

Apply the stencil in the usual way and begin to airbrush the berries red. Adjust the flow of colour so that it is very specific in its direction.

~ 2 ~

Change the colour to leaf green and colour the leaves over the rest of the stencil. Check very thoroughly that nothing has been missed.

~ 3 ~

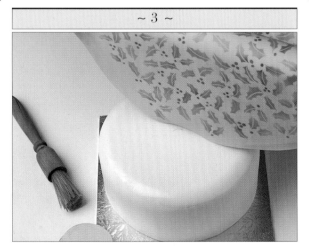

Moisten the surface of the cake with clear alcohol, masking the appropriate areas. Carefully transfer the patterned sheet to the top of the cake.

~ 4 ~

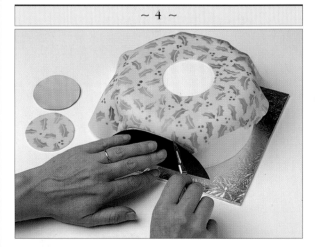

Divide the cake into 6 equal sections and cut the arches around the sides using a circular template. Also remove a circle from the centre.

CHRISTMAS TRIMMINGS

*Y*ou can use the stencils designed for the Christmas cake to make a greeting card and trimmings. The trimmings are quick and simple to make. I have used a combination of plain and scalloped circular cutters to make the tree decorations. Children can have great fun making the trimmings, which can be varnished if you want to keep them indefinitely. The quantity of stencilling paste below is sufficient to make a selection of these items.

*375g (12 oz) ivory-coloured Stencilling Paste,
see page 6
white vegetable fat (shortening)
gum tragacanth
poinsettia red and leaf green liquid food
colourings
dark gold dusting powder (petal dust/
blossom tint)
clear alcohol (gin or vodka)
small amount of Royal Icing, see page 6*

E Q U I P M E N T

*airbrush
plain circular cutters
Garrett frill cutter
piping bag
small pieces of foam sponge
thick flexible card
adhesive tape
red ribbon
carnation cutter*

● To strengthen the stencilling paste, knead a small amount of gum tragacanth into it before making the decorations, card and napkin rings.

CHRISTMAS TREE DECORATIONS

❖

● These decorations have been made in exactly the same way as the card and napkin rings. They are all made from a double thickness of stencilling paste. This gives them more body and enables you to secure a small piece of ribbon in between the two with royal icing, so that they can be hung from the tree.

● The possibilities for variations are endless – simply use a range of suitable cutters and experiment to create your own stylish decorations. Many different-shaped cutters are available, including square, oval, heart and star.

NAPKIN RINGS

❖

Cut out six pieces of card, about 15 x 5cm (6 x 2 in). Roll each one into a tubular shape and secure with adhesive tape. To make the napkin rings, cut out six 15 x 5cm (6 x 2 in) pieces of patterned paste. Wrap each one round a card ring, overlapping at the join. Secure with clear alcohol. Leave to dry. Trim with gold edging.

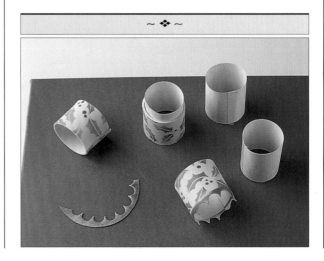

GREETING CARD

❖

Decorate a full sheet of stencilling paste with the holly pattern as described on page 56. Cut out the stencilling paste to the required size for the front and back of the card. Use a small plain circular cutter and cut out the centre of the front of the card. Leave to dry thoroughly.

Trim with a thin strip of gold-coloured stencilling paste cut with a Garrett frill cutter and secure with clear alcohol. Make up the stencilled section, as described in the step-by-step instructions, to decorate inside the card. If you wish to add a greeting, it too needs to be done at this stage. Secure the front and back of the card together with royal icing.

EXPERT ADVICE

≈

Be careful not to overwet the paste when the trimming is attached or it will smudge the painted stencilled surface.

There are other ways in which this stencil can be used, including, for example wrapping a section around a cake as a border design. It can also be applied in a similar way to the Tiered Wedding Cake, see page 46, and, if used on a very thin layer of stencilling paste, it can be draped over the surface of the cake to create the effect of fabric.

~ 1 ~

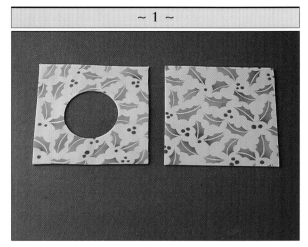

Cut out both the front and back of the card. The card shown is about 12cm (4½ in) square. While the paste is still wet, use a small plain circular cutter to cut out the front. If you do not have one, a card template can be used.

~ 2 ~

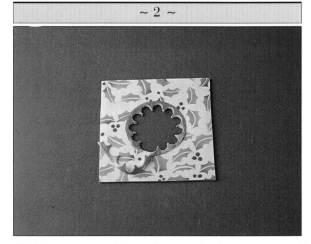

Roll out a thin sheet of ivory-coloured stencilling paste and dust the surface dark gold. Cut out Garrett frill sections and use to trim the edge of the circle, securing with clear alcohol.

STENCILLED SUGAR BOX

This box has been made in white and soft pastel colours.

5ml (1 tsp) gum tragacanth
1kg (2 lb) Stencilling Paste, see page 6
white vegetable fat (shortening)
clear alcohol (gin or vodka)
peach paste food colouring
*holly and ivy green, marigold, poinsettia
and white dusting powders (petal dusts/
blossom tints)*
small amount of Royal Icing, see page 6
EQUIPMENT
50 x 7.5cm (20 x 3 in) thick card
Garrett frill cutter
stencil film
tissue paper
adhesive tape
piping bag

● Knead the gum tragacanth into the paste. This will give the box a little extra strength. First make the lid for the sugar box by following the instructions on page 64.

● Prepare to make the sugar box. Cut a strip of card long enough to form a ring of the same diameter as the stencil, see page 64. Secure the

---

EXPERT ADVICE

≈

You may find that you have a pot or dish of a suitable size around which the side of the sugar box may be moulded; in which case there is no need to cut a ring of card.

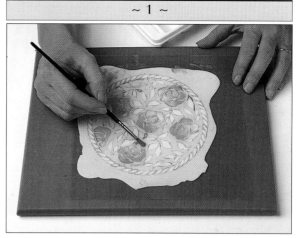

1

Roll out and apply 125g (4 oz) stencilling paste to the stencil in the usual way. Dust part of the roses in marigold. Change colour to a soft pink and overdust the flower to create a two-tone effect.

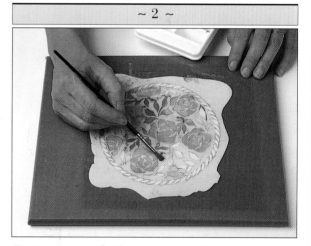

Dust some of the leaves with a touch of marigold and overdust with holly and ivy green. Dust the border in holly and ivy green. Cut away the white areas between the flowers and trim around the edge.

card in a ring shape with adhesive tape: it should be about 15cm (6 in) in diameter but it is important to check the diameter of the ring with the stencil for the lid as it will be used to dry the side of the box.

● Make each section of the box, following the step-by-step instructions and leave to dry thoroughly before assembling. When the box is completely dry, line it with tissue paper and fill with Turkish delight or sweets of your choice.

STORING AND FILLING THE BOX

Do not store the box with the lid on: line the lid with a shallow circle of foam sponge to prevent it from sagging and store it separately. Any dampness or a very humid atmosphere can cause the lid the sag.

Remember, too, that moist sweets will also cause the box to soften and sag. When packing confectionery such as Turkish delight in the box as a gift, place it in an airtight polythene bag if it is to be left for any length of time.

Box Lid
Enlarge to 123 per cent
on a photocopier

~ 1 ~

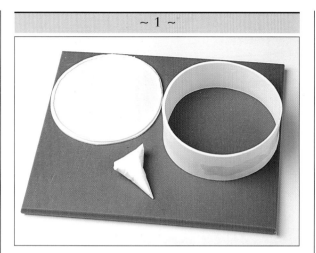

MAKING THE BOX *Roll out 90g (3 oz) stencilling paste 3mm (⅛ in) thick. Use the card ring to cut out a circle of paste for the box base. Cut a strip of 3mm (⅛ in) thick stencilling paste and trim to fit around the card ring for the box side. Secure the ends with royal icing; if necessary, stick the join with tape. Leave to dry. Remove the ring of paste from the card, discarding any tape. Pipe royal icing around the circumference of the base and position the ring carefully. Tidy the join if necessary. Leave to dry.*

EXPERT ADVICE

≈

I have slightly overestimated the amount of stencilling paste needed as it is important that the pieces are thicker than normal.

~ 2 ~

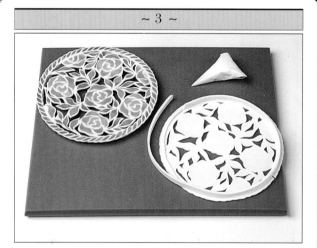

Roll out 140g (4½ oz) of peach-coloured stencilling paste and cut a strip and circle to fit inside the box. Line the box with these sections, securing them with clear alcohol. Use a lace cutter to cut a strip of peach paste and use to trim the outside of the box.

~ 3 ~

Turn the lid upside down and lightly score a ring just smaller than the inside circumference of the box. Roll out a long, narrow strip of 3mm (⅛ in) thick stencilling paste and trim to fit around the scored line. Secure with royal icing. This is the lid rim to fit inside the box.

TEMPLATES

Stencilling with Royal Icing, see page 25

Kite Cake, see page 14

Valentine's Cake, see page 16

Bumble Bees and Daisies:
Side Decoration, see page 51

Stencilled Strawberries, see page 38

Bumble Bees and Daisies:
Side Decoration, see page 51

Right *Daffodil Cake:*
Side Decoration, see page 20

Unusual Christmas Cake,
see page 55

Daffodil Cake,
see page 20

An Outrageous Birthday Cake, see page 42
Enlarge by 126 per cent on a photocopier

An Outrageous Birthday
Cake, see page 42

Enlarge by 126 per cent on a photocopier

INDEX

FOR FURTHER INFORMATION

Merehurst is the leading publisher of cake decorating books and has an excellent range of titles to suit cake decorators of all levels. Please send for a free catalogue, stating the title of this book:

United Kingdom
Marketing Department
Merehurst Ltd.
Ferry House
51 – 57 Lacy Road
London SW15 1PR
Tel: 0181 780 1177
Fax: 0181 780 1714

U.S.A./Canada
Foxwood International Ltd.
150 Nipissing Road # 6
Milton
Ontario L9T 5B2
Canada
Tel: 0101 905 875 4040
Fax: 0101 905 875 1668

Australia
Herron Book Distributors
91 Main Street
Kangaroo Point
Queensland 4169
Australia
Tel: 010 61 7 891 2866
Fax: 010 61 7 891 2909

Other Territories
For further information
contact:
International Sales
Department at United
Kingdom address.